# 8th Grade Middle School Chronicles

# 8th Grade Middle School Chronicles

**The year that changed everything...**

Written by

**Essynce E. Moore**

8th Grade Middle School Chronicles

write to:
## Essynce Couture Publishing
## P.O. BOX 5082
## Hillside, NJ 07205

Printed in the United States of America

Published by Essynce Couture Publishing

Hillside, NJ 07205

Editor: Essynce Couture Publishing

Cover Photo: Essynce Moore

Photographer: I.C.U. HD Photography

Cover Design: Jamar Hargrove – Owner of NeedGFX.com

**Essynce E. Moore**
Entrepreneur, Motivational Speaker, Actress, Author, Fashion Designer, & Stylist, Founder and CEO of Essynce Couture, LLC, Essynce Couture University, and Essynce Couture Spa and Boutique

www.essyncecouture.com

ISBN-13: 978-0692872932 (Custom Universal)
ISBN-10: 0692872930

Printed in USA by Essynce Couture Publishing

Essynce E. Moore

# Table of Contents:

Introduction

Chapter 1.................................................................

"The First Day"

Chapter 2.................................................................

"Throwing A Punch"

Chapter 3.................................................................

"Momentarily Losing My Mind"

Chapter 4.................................................................

"One of the Guys"

Chapter 5.................................................................

"One of the Worst Mistakes I'd Ever Made…"

Chapter 6.................................................................

"I'll Just Pretend That One Didn't Sting…"

Chapter 7.................................................................

"I'm Fine."

Chapter 8.................................................................

"Surprise!"

Chapter 9.....................................................................

"Nothing Could Bring Me Down…"

Chapter 10...................................................................

"Thanks A Lot Cinnamon"

Chapter 11...................................................................

"This Generation Is A Walking Petty Party"

Chapter 12...................................................................

"I Have No Choice Other Than To…"

Chapter 13...................................................................

"A GTA God"

Chapter 14...................................................................

"Friends"

Chapter 15...................................................................

"I'm So Different."

Chapter 16...................................................................

"Honestly"

## Introduction:

When the worst thing a 13-year-old girl could imagine happens what does she do? Does she...

A. Write a book
B. Freak out!
C. Take a deep breath and says, "On the bright side this will make a very entertaining chapter."

The answer is... all of the above! Now I know what you're probably thinking, that wasn't even an answer choice. But that pretty much describes how my 8th grade year went. The correct answer never seemed to be the choice right in front of me. Sometimes what appears to be right, so obvious, could be entirely, downright wrong. I said it in my last book and I'll say it again. Expect the Unexpected!

Essynce E. Moore

# Chapter 1:
# "The First Day"

# Chapter 1
## *"The First Day"*

*T*he first day of school I wore burgundy jeans, a grey button down shirt, a grey and burgundy tie, and black sneakers. I wore gold jewelry and had a fresh haircut on the shaved side of my head. Oh, and I had blue hair. It was the first of many colors to come! I also had the book bag of my dreams. It was a Sprayground bookbag and on it was a blue unicorn with a bunch of tattoos and gold piercings. The horn was gold as well and it was made with metal material to give the bag more of a 3D effect. On the unicorn's forehead read a tattoo that said *"Born This Way."* That bag was my baby! I remember having left over pizza for breakfast and thinking this was going to be a good day. I was finally the oldest in my class. I was in a school that ranged from 6th-8th grade and I was finally an 8th grader! The guppy was now a shark!

Once my mom dropped me off to school I made my way towards the playground area where everyone would meet until it was time to go inside. There, I ran into my friends. We all made small talk about what everyone did over the summer and everyone kept asking me if my septum nose piercing was real. I had to keep saying it wasn't. As I looked around the playground I saw a bunch of new faces, most of them were attached to small bodies signifying they were indeed 6<sup>th</sup> graders. Some of them looked lost and confused, while others mingled with the 7<sup>th</sup> graders. It all gave me a huge sense of déjà vu.

When it was time to go inside we all went to homeroom. That's where I received my schedule and what I saw surprised me. I was in all honors classes! The classes being honors science, social studies, reading, and *algebra*. I was confident in all my classes but the one subject that always seemed to frustrate, confuse, and upset me was math. *I hated math*, I still do. I looked at the *Honors Algebra* printed upon the piece of paper, as my first period class, repeatedly just to be sure I was seeing things correctly and the more I stared at it, the more I began to feel insecure. I could already imagine myself sitting at a wooden desk in class with a question mark above my head as I glanced upon some unfeasible equation. To be honest math stopped being easy for me when they started putting letters in equations.

That's when the morning announcements came on bringing me out of my trance. The voice coming out of the speaker that hung above the classroom door was unfamiliar. It wasn't until the voice gave us a name and title that we found out who it belonged to, our new principal Mr. Lopez. In that moment, we were all reminded that our old principal Mr. Parker, had retired.

Everyone in the class just looked at one-another as the realization sunk in, things were going to change. We all knew that much, but we weren't sure just how different things would become.

Mr. Lopez went over some rules and regulations, a lot of them had to do with the uniform. By the time he was finished everyone, including myself, groaned in frustration. It was only the first day and somehow everyone was already put into a bad mood.

# Notes:

Essynce E. Moore

# Chapter 2: "Throwing A Punch"

# Chapter 2
## *"Throwing A Punch"*

**A** couple weeks had gone by and everyone seemed to be finding their own way to work around all the new changes and rearrangements. We weren't your ideal school but we sure were making progress, at least I thought we were. That was until late September, there was a fight.

The fight took place after school, in front of the corner store, only a few feet away from the school building. My mom was parked across the street waiting to pick up my best friend Amy and I. There was a huge crowd of kids pushing and shoving one-another to get a good view of the fight. I grabbed Amy's hand and tried to maneuver our way around our shouting classmates. Meanwhile Amy was trying to persuade me to stay and watch the fight. I tuned her out, which was simple with all the yelling going on, and I made our way across the street towards my mom's silver Lexus.

I never understood the thrill or interest in watching people fight. Neither participant truly comes out a winner and most of the time people are fighting because of the attention they're receiving from the audience. People who are labeled "nobodies" automatically become "somebodies" for what? Throwing a punch?

*Impressive.*

When people fought in my school everyone saw it as entertainment. I saw it as not being emotionally or physically capable of handling conflicts with words. Call me crazy but I thought violence should always be the last resort while many of my peers saw it as the holy grail of problem solving.

Anyway, I'm losing focus. When Amy and I got to my mother she was already getting out of the car. Her view from across the street gave her a clear understanding as to what was going on. As the fight broke out children were being pushed into the street and hopping on one-another's backs just to see the action.

*"People should mind their business,"* I thought.

My mom started making her way across the street and all it took were 5 words to come out of her mouth for all of my friends who were watching the fight to make their way across the street towards Amy and I.

"All mine across the street!" My mother yelled.

In that moment, everyone who had ever been in my house, accompanied me somewhere, or knew my mom personally made their way across the street. My mom had to help some of my smaller friends get through the crowd. Amy and I were amused at how everyone knew exactly who they were when my mom referred to them as "hers."

Soon there was a good 14 of us across the street. That included me and my friends Cece, Alice, Mike, Mia, Chris, Ian, Faith, Amy, Zach, Angel, and Jazzy. However, one of us was still missing and there he was across the street, in the crowd, yelling and chanting with the rest of the frycks. Mike pointed him out to my mom and she muttered an irritated "of course" when she saw that he was still watching the fight. It was "The Flame," the mischievous guy I'd had a crush on since 7th grade. There he was jumping and screaming along with the rest of my peers.

My mom went across the street once more to retrieve the final fryck who protested being pulled away from all the action. She ignored his pleas and pulled him by his ear towards us just like all the moms did in the movies. It was quite comedic actually. All of us laughed uncontrollably and when they'd finally reached us, with my mom still holding onto his ear, he greeted us by saying "hey guys!" He waved enthusiastically with a big grin on his face like he'd enjoyed all the effort and attention required to bring him across the street to join the rest of us. His grin possessed the same innocence a child would have when acting as if they'd done nothing wrong when they obviously did. To be honest you'd expect some halo to shine above his head based off his expression. But we all knew "The Flame" and he was no angel. That was conclusive, and not up for discussion.

When it was all over the cops had shown up and my mom dropped some of my friends off at home, or to whatever practice they had that day for football or cheerleading. When we were finally alone she told me that she couldn't believe that's what happens during fights these day, everyone watching and cheering. I couldn't say anything, that had become the norm in my generation. All I could do was mind my own business.

# Notes:

# Chapter 3:

# "Momentarily Losing My Mind"

# Chapter 3

## *"Momentarily Losing My Mind!"*

*J* want to say it was in October that I'd lost it in my honor's algebra class. Confusion had managed to turn to oblivion and I felt horrible. It was like my eyes would muster up the courage to look at equations written on the board, and the minute I'd try to solve one my brain would go into malfunction! My head would start to pound signifying a headache was approaching and I'd get incredibly insecure.

When I'd rip my eyes away from my worksheet, not being able to stand the sight of it anymore, my eyes would meet the view of my classmates who happened to be all the smart kids. Now don't get me wrong, I knew I was intelligent and I knew I was put in that class for a reason. My 7th grade math teacher wanted to challenge me seeing as I usually approached challenges really well, but this was different. I felt *dumb* and it sucked because when I occasionally snuck glances at the other students that surrounded me they all seemed so focused and knowledgeable at what they were doing. Meanwhile, here I was momentarily losing my mind!

My mom always taught me to ask questions if there was something I didn't understand so I did, lots of times. I even went after school for extra help for crying out loud! The sound of the thick accent my teacher had, rang in my ears like an alarm.

"MAY DATE, MAY DATE WHAT HE'S ABOUT TO SAY WILL MAKE NO SENSE! I REPEAT WHAT HE'S ABOUT TO SAY WILL MAKE NO SENSE! THIS IS NOT A DRILL!"

You see the problem wasn't even his accent, it was the words he'd use to form sentences that were supposed to help me understand, but just didn't. It was like my mind was mentally incapable of comprehending algebra 1.

Then there would be that split second of satisfaction when I think I'd finally understand how to solve for x. In that very appreciated moment I would answer an equation and my answer would be...wrong! I couldn't win and that's when I started thinking is there really anything worth winning here? When in my life will I need to know how to solve for x and y? The way we learned things in school you'd think speed limit signs would have some equation and "SOLVE FOR X" written in big bold letters beneath it! No, that is not the way society works people! I mean come on!

Alright, let me take a moment to breathe because I've begun stabbing my keyboard with my fingers while typing this which isn't exactly a good thing. I'm using my mom's laptop... *inhales/exhales*

Okay, I feel much better. Now let's get to the part when I conquered my demons and rode off into the sunset!

I informed my mom about struggling in math. It wasn't up until she saw my grades that she emailed the principal to try and come up with a solution to solve my predicament. All my grades were either A's or B's but in my honors algebra class I had a D.

*Well I can't say I didn't try.*

Anyway, that D needed to change. The marking period would be over in about a month and I needed to make honor roll, not for my mom or my teachers, but for myself.

One day I got called to the principal's office. I knew I wasn't in trouble and I knew what we'd be discussing, my algebra class. What I didn't know is my algebra teacher would be waiting for me in his office as well.

*What a lovely surprise.*

Mr. Lopez explained to me that as a child he couldn't comprehend the meaning or use of a Venn diagram. You know, those compare and contrast circles we use mostly in language arts. I looked at Mr. Lopez like he was crazy. I mean the concept was so simple and direct. Yet, he didn't understand it and he informed me that I shouldn't be so hard on myself about not being able to understand something. That's' just life. Next, Mr. Lopez told me that if I wanted I could transfer into a regular math class and I agreed to do so.

At first I was kind of upset. I felt like I had given up, but once I entered regular math and came face to face with some of my goofy friends I knew I would be fine. I ended up being one of the smartest in my class too! Oh, and I made honor roll with an A in math.

So that my friends is how I conquered **one** of my demons. Believe me, there will be plenty more to come.

# Notes:

Essynce E. Moore

# Chapter 4: "One of the Guys"

# Chapter 4
## *"One of the Guys"*

𝐽t was now fall, during the cool winds football season had approached. It was a season that seemed to bring everyone out of the house in my hometown, including me.

I had a lot of friends who played the game, and the time we usually spend hanging out at our community center turned into their football practice. At first, I was a little bummed. You see, over the summer and in the very beginning of the school year I always hung out with my guy friends at the community center, but when football season started I knew they'd be loaded with practice. At least I thought they would be. That is until we found a solution to our little problem.

Football practice started around 6:00 PM and ended around 7:30 PM. My curfew was at 8 so I had to be home by then. I showed up to the community center, also known as the PAL at about 5 "o" clock. My friends would be there early before practice and in the meantime, they would teach me how to play and it was really fun!

My friend Jonas and I were really close, and he along with 3 other of my guy friends taught me how to throw, tackle, and score a touchdown. I started playing well and loved watching the ball spiral in the air when I threw it. The guys and I would play all kinds of games like throw-ups or see who could throw the farthest. I had grown to have a small yet vivid love for football, or maybe it was just the new exhilaration I felt when I had gotten an opportunity to be active and play rough for once, seeing as I was never really a physical person. That didn't matter though. All I knew was, I was having fun!

There would be times when we'd play really rough, and when those times came I would be the one doing most of the tackling. I was incredibly impressed with how exceptional I've gotten playing, but the one person I could never beat was Jonas. He was a football God, undeniably amazing! No one could beat him, and no one underestimated me because I was a girl. I was "one of the guys" when I was with them. In fact, I had run over more guys than I could count, and one of them just so happened to be a star player on the team. I hadn't even noticed till I turned around, after making a touchdown, to find all of my friends surrounding the guy who I had tackled on the ground. Everyone laughed, including him, and I couldn't help but laugh myself.

Essynce, the fashion designer and honor roll student had ran over a much bigger and much stronger football player.

*Never underestimate me!*

After a couple of weeks I had developed a system. I walked home from school, changed into some sweatpants and a hoodie, and went to the community center. When practiced started and my friends had to go I watched them play. When practice ended my best friend Zach, who played on the team, would walk me home since he passed my house on his way. My mom never let me walk home alone when it got dark.

When I watched my friends play their coach would yell an infamous amount of commands and complaints such as, "FASTER! HURRY UP! WHAT'S TAKING YOU SO LONG?"

I would sit on a small hill where everyone would place their bags and water bottles, and simply observe. Watching them play fascinated me. There was so much that went into every distance they would run and every length they'd go to achieve their goal. It was inspiring. Like I said before, it was fall, so somedays it was really cold, but I would stay and watch anyway. Sometimes while the guys were practicing I'd go to the store down the street and get my friends drinks. I would get Zach a fruit punch Arizona, Jonas an iced tea, and on a good day

I'd get "The Flame" a drink too. Did I forget to mention he played as well? Well he did and he challenged me when we'd play together, forcing me to run faster and shove harder. It was annoying at first but I grew to like it.

Sometimes, while the guys would run laps they'd pass me and "The Flame" would gently hit me, then keep running almost as a reminder to pay attention to him on the field. I'd laugh and occasionally their coach would come over and talk to me, asking how the team was doing. I guess he asked me because I was always there on the sidelines watching. At first, I was surprised because he seemed so aggressive and serious while coaching which is his job I guess, but I gave him my advice anyway. I told him that he should call on some of the guys and tell them what they need to work on individually, and he would nod his head and contemplate my advice before taking it. He was actually a pretty nice guy, and I later found out that he was one of my friend's parents.

There was this one time the coach called me over when the team huddled up together, and I got a up close, and personal view on what it is guys talked about when they'd finish practice.

*Girls.*

The coach basically told the guys that now was the time for them to have multiple girlfriends since that all changes when they get married. I found his advice...amusing. I mean it was such a *guy* thing to say, I couldn't help but chuckle a little. That's when this kid James cut in on the action and said that after every game the girls were always all over him. He even put his hand on his hip and spoke in a high pitch voice.

"Oh my god! James, you played so well today, no wonder you're the quarterback!" He said imitating what his take on the girl's compliments usually were after he played.

It was hilarious! James was a great player. He was the quarterback, and he just so happened to be in the 9$^{th}$ grade.

There was this one time when Jonas had me throw a football in front of James to show him how good I was. Once I threw the ball it flew a great distance reaching the middle of the field and Jonas yelled behind me... "She's coming for your position as quarterback James!"

James looked at me and my throw with admiration. Afterwards he laughed at Jonas' comment and nodded his head in agreement. He then turned to me with a kind smile. I had to admit, James wasn't exactly bad on the eyes if you know what I mean.

About a week had gone by and everything was pretty much still the same. I'd leave school, go home and change, play with the guys, and when practiced ended Zach would walk me home. Sometimes Zach would take his time getting his stuff together before we began walking and I'd have to remind him that I needed to be home by 8. It would get annoying after a while because Zach wouldn't be done changing out of his equipment until about 7:50 PM. There would be times when he wanted to stay and watch people play basketball on the court, and I'd be running late.  I did not want to miss my curfew and I couldn't walk home alone either, that was even worse in my mom's eyes.

One day, Zach had me waiting for him till 7:55!  I didn't live super far but I would still need to run to make it home on time and I had to walk by myself because Zack refused to leave the PAL.  So, there I was walking home in the dark by myself.  I was angry and upset with Zach. I thought to myself... "Why couldn't Zach just walk me home? Why did he have to be so difficult?"

# Notes:

---------------

# Chapter 5:

# "One of the Worst Mistakes I'd Ever Made..."

---------------

# Chapter 5
## *"One of the Worst Mistakes I'd Ever Made…"*

*I* hadn't spoken to Zach after the incident, and it was a lot harder than I thought. He was my best friend and I practically told him everything!

One day in health class, Zach tried getting my attention by throwing paper balls at me. I just ignored his attempts and one of my close friends Alice asked me if I was mad at him. I just shrugged my shoulders and didn't respond. Meanwhile, Alice looked incredibly surprised. Usually the 3 of us would be having some hilarious conversation that would make absolutely no sense, but there I was refusing to talk to Zach. I may have overexaggerated but I just kept thinking back to that moment I was in the dark alone, walking by myself all because Zach didn't want to leave the PAL.

When I got home from school that day I told my mom about what had happened and she gave me her advice. She told me that Zach was a great best friend. She knew because he was always around, accompanying me at my events and helping out when he could, and it was because he was such a great friend that this fight wasn't worth ending our friendship over. At least that's what she thought and I couldn't help but agree. So, the next day after health class I spoke to Zach and told him how I felt about the whole situation. If I didn't do that and continued being mad at him I can honestly say that would have been one of the worst mistakes I would have ever made. Zach is still my best friend today, and there are times I don't know what I'd do without him.

My advice for anyone ever in a similar situation is to just think "is this really worth losing a friend over?"

# Notes:

---

# Chapter 6:
# "I'll Just Pretend That One Didn't Sting..."

---

# Chapter 6:
## *"I'll Just Pretend That One Didn't Sting..."*

*O*ne day, just like any other, I went to school. During lunch I sat with my usual group of friends and went about my normal routine. At some point I ended up having to use the bathroom so I did the traditional "girl thing to do" and asked Mia, who happened to be one of my closest friends, if she wanted to come with me. She agreed. As we got up to leave our table I remember seeing "The Flame" staring at us out of the corner of my eye, almost as if he knew something I didn't.

After I did my business, I made my way over to the sink to wash my hands where Mia stood looking in the mirror fixing her hair. That's when she turned to me and said, "I need to tell you something."

"Me too, it's about something that happened yesterday, but you go first." I responded, while running my hands beneath the cold water. The warm water never worked in my school.

"The Flame" was talking about what happened at the PAL the other day."

"What are you talking about?" I had an idea as to what Mia was getting at but I wanted to hear her say it just to be sure.

"The almost kiss thing."

Yea, I knew exactly where she was going with this...

**\*\*\*\*\*FLASHBACK\*\*\*\*\***

I'm gonna assume it was a Wednesday or Thursday when I almost had my first kiss. I had gone to the PAL after school and ended up hanging out with my troublemaking friends Dre, "The Flame", and DJ who I happened to love dearly.

It started to get a little late and the guys would always play this irritating game with me when they wanted to either irk my nerves or get me to stay at the PAL longer. It was a game that would seem to come up the most right when I was about to leave the PAL. They would take my phone, the one thing I can't leave the PAL without, and toss it amongst one-another. I had a protective case so it's not like my phone would break if they dropped it, but that wasn't their intention to begin with. See, I never knew which of them *had* my phone. It could be Dre, DJ, or the ring-leader who just so happened to be the guy I liked, "The Flame." They would exchange my phone amongst the 3 of them without me even seeing who it had been given to. I thought it was DJ one minute and "The Flame" would have it the next. It was childish and they knew that, but I think they secretly liked watching me suffer.

They laughed as I tried to retrieve my cellular device, and I would try to be serious only to make the mistake of laughing, blowing my own cover. When the game had finally come to an end Dre and DJ disappeared off into the basketball court leaving "The Flame" and I alone outside. By then, I had forgotten all about leaving the PAL. Their little plan had worked once again.

"The Flame" and I sat on some of the equipment beneath the jungle gym and just talked. He said his head was starting to hurt and I couldn't help but feel bad. His playful demeanor had vanished and I could tell that he was in pain. I placed the palm of my hand on his head and came to the conclusion that he was pretty warm. I began massaging his temples like I had done for myself when I had headaches. He, in response towards my actions, closed his eyes and seemed satisfied with the newly found pressure against him. When I stopped, he opened his eyes and just looked at me. I don't think I could ever really describe the expression he was wearing upon his face, but that's when he had begun pulling the hoodie I was wearing towards him. Right when I was about to reach his lips I pulled away. I don't remember why...I just did. I know I was nervous, everything was great and I couldn't help but suspect something would go wrong so I had to go and ruin things. At least I thought I'd spoiled everything. In my mind, I had chickened out of my first kiss.

**\*\*\*\*\*End of Flashback\*\*\*\*\***

"What are you talking about?"

"The almost kiss thing."

My heart raced in anticipation for Mia to continue. I was calm on the outside and borderline freaking out on the inside!

"What did he say?" I asked.

"You sure you wanna know?" Mia seemed nervous about telling me which only seemed to build my curiosity.

"Positive."

"He told Amy and I that he knew you were gonna tell us about what happened yesterday, so he told us that he was never going to kiss you. He said that if he wanted to he would have."

"Oh."

*I'll just pretend that one didn't sting.*

"You okay?"

*No, not really.*

"Yea I'm fine." I responded.

*Lie.*

"Okay good."

"Yea, I think it's about time I got over him anyway."

*Another lie.*

"I agree." Mia stated smiling.

 

      While walking back to the cafeteria I thought about how I would react to what "The Flame" said to Mia because I believed every word she said. It explained why he was looking at Mia and I all weird before we left. It was like he knew she was going to tell me, which she did. I remembered thinking "so how am I going to do this?"

*Should I give him the silent treatment?*

*Should I confront him about it?*

And that's when I decided that I was going to play the *"I don't care, it doesn't affect me card"* when in reality it did. It actually hurt quite a bit.

      When we got to our table "The Flame" was staring at me intently as if he was looking for some sign of anger or sadness, two emotions I happened to be a master at hiding. So, there I was playing the "I don't care card" and everyone was buying it. I laughed at all their jokes and acted as if the sun were shining when in reality I felt like it were a tsunami outside.

*Another* day. *Another* demon.

# Notes:

# Chapter 7: "I'm Fine"

# Chapter 7
## *"I'm Fine."*

About a week had gone by and I had gotten over the "almost kiss" incident. I hadn't forgotten what happened but I sure pretended it didn't. I had done what I always did, come up with an excuse for him, make up some justifiable reason as to why he did what he did. I told myself that maybe he was telling the truth, maybe I had been reading things wrong the entire time, but in the back of my mind I couldn't help but replay the moment in my head over and over again. I could've sworn that he was going to kiss me. It was late, the moon was out, it was just the two of us, I *knew* he was going to. Yet, I pushed that thought away because it seemed to only make things worse by allowing myself to care, so I convinced myself that I was wrong. I treated him as I normally would and went about my day.

Meanwhile, everyone around me assumed I was over the whole thing. Why did they think this? Because that's what I told them and they bought every word. All the while I was waiting for someone to see past that lie and acknowledge or at least take some notice in how I really felt.

But things were different this time around. Something had changed with the people I considered my friends, that sat with me at the lunch table, two friends in particular, "The Flame" and Mia.

Mia had been one of my best friends since 6th grade, and in the three years we had grown to know one-another we were inseparable. I invited her to *everything*. We had gone to Atlanta, Georgia with one-another and ended up sneaking into a Lady GaGa concert. We had more sleepovers and get togethers than I could count, we were partners for multiple school projects, we borrowed each other's clothes, stored stuff in each other's lockers, we even planned our future adventures together. She was my sister. Now you're probably wondering why I told you all this, and that is to help you understand the story I'm about to tell and why it affected me the way it did.

Put yourself in my shoes and join me as I tell a very important story. Live through it with me and allow yourself to feel how I had felt when it all went down.


Here we go...


*About a week or two later after Mia had told me what "The Flame" supposedly said, she confessed* something to me. The confession being she liked him and at first I couldn't blame her. How could I? He was like rain in a desert, guys like him didn't come around too often, one of a kind for sure.

When Mia told me the news for the first time I had begun to notice the constant flirting between them, and every day at lunch they'd sit directly across from me flirting and laughing. It sucked. I continuously told myself I didn't care and I hoped that because I told myself I didn't one day that would actually be the case.

Soon one of my famous weekly movie nights was approaching and it was perfect timing. We didn't have school on Thursday or Friday so my movie night was placed on a semi-cold November, Wednesday night, @6:00pm. I went to the PAL to spread the word and a bunch of people showed up. There were so many of us and so many people turning up at my door that one of my guy friends had to step in and tell the kids outside that there was no more room. My living room space was limited for sure. Anyway, while we searched for a movie to watch I couldn't help but notice "The Flame" and Mia side-by-side on my couch.

When we could all agree on a movie I squeezed onto my couch. Some people were sitting on the floor with blankets and pillows and all of us chowed down on popcorn. It was nearly perfect, except...it wasn't. This movie night was different, things usually went smoothly and accordingly, but with all the teenage bodies in my house, with my mother upstairs in her room everyone was doing something different. There were people on their phones during the movie which never really happened at my movie nights and there was a bunch of talking. No one was really paying attention to the TV screen and that was never a problem before. That wasn't even the worse part.

We haven't gotten there yet...

The worse part was "The Flame" and Mia would not stop flirting! It could be a hand, a thigh, or even a shoulder that managed to connect them together, allowing them to touch. Of course, I saw this. Finally, I went upstairs to use the bathroom and when I came back down I couldn't help but notice that "The Flame" and Mia were missing. I went in my kitchen for a snack and there they were...

She was pressed against my fridge with his body pressed against hers. They were about to kiss.

What could I say? What could I do to make myself pretend I didn't care? Apparently pretending not to care was a game I had grown accustomed to playing. Everything had become a game. It was like there was an unspoken competition that everyone knew about but never said out loud.

Who could go the longest without being affected?

Who could turn it into a joke?

Who could pretend nothing hurt and hide their feelings the longest?

It was all a game and I hated it! Yet I still played along because...I don't know why, I just did. That's what everyone else was doing.

So, I did the only thing I knew how to do...I played along. I used every ounce of control I had over myself left and forced a laugh to escape my mouth.

"Jeez guys, I just wanted a snack." I said.

I didn't want it anymore.

They looked at me with goofy grins and I forced myself to mirror the same expression.

He flirts with girls all the time.

*I'm used to this.*

*It's No.Big.Deal.*

*Then why are you sad? I heard a voice say in the back of my mind and my response was I'm fine.*

*Great now I'm talking to myself, I thought.*


I couldn't wait for everyone to leave. I wanted to be alone. I wanted to "not care" by myself, in my room, on my bed, into my pillow. I don't know how I lasted until they all left but I did and when they were gone...I broke.

I went into my room, laid down on my bed, and told myself I couldn't "not care" anymore. I did care and because I cared so much I cried my eyes out. Everything hurt, my heart, my head, my whole body hurt. It all hit me at once. Every girl he ever flirted with in front of me, every long hour he ever took to text me back, and that moment with him and my "sister" about to kiss in my kitchen on my fridge with my first love. It was painful, a heartbreak at its finest.

That's when I realized I couldn't handle this pain on my own, so I called my cousin, who was my real sister. She sounded so happy on the other end of the phone while talking to her mom, my aunt, in the background and when she turned her attention to me I didn't know what to say. I was feeling so many things at once, jealousy, anger, **sadness**, that one seemed to stick out the most. So, I said two words that felt incredibly heavy to push out of my mouth. It was like refusing to admit how I actually felt for so long made it so difficult to say the truth.

"I'm fine" was all I had come to know.

"I'm sad" was what I said for the first time in a long time.

In half-a-second my sister was concerned. I told her what happened and she consoled me over the phone for about an hour, and gave me advice that I don't remember but I do remember it helping.

For a few days I didn't talk much. All the talking was done in my head. There were times I would blame myself for him not liking me. I thought I wasn't enough, never could be, and never would be. Then an hour later I told myself I was better off without him, and those emotions would take turns rolling around in my head and in my heart. It was all so very confusing and it was all a part of my first heartbreak. I never had another movie night after that one. I was never the same after that day. I never looked at my "friends" the same. I never looked at myself the same. Like I said...I broke and I never found all my pieces. I just learned to work with what I had, and that got me to writing this. So, I guess we're not at a total loss.

I mean this is only chapter seven...

# Notes:

Essynce E. Moore

# Chapter 8: "Surprise!"

# Chapter 8
## *"Surprise!"*

𝕵t was now December. Life seemed to have no choice but to go on. Not a day went by I hadn't thought of that Wednesday night at least once, but I had to be patient, things take time. Getting over someone takes time.

Meanwhile, I developed a liking towards a certain singing group, <u>The Digz</u>. I always found my way to their concerts, and I couldn't help but fangirl over one of the singers. His name was Tevin and he was 15 and undeniably attractive. There were three guys in the group and they were great singers. Some of the girls at my school thought so too. The singing group even made an appearance at my store's grand-opening back in November. A week before the opening I spoke to Tevin's mom, who was their manager, about who I was and the boys coming to show their faces at my store. A couple of concerts later they were there at my grand-opening. It was all kinds of amazing!

It was the very beginning of December when I went to another one of their concerts and they remembered me! We made small talk while they met other fans, and then there was a raffle. My friend Jackie, who accompanied me to the concert, bought five raffle tickets as did I. The prize was a date with the boys. There would be three winners who each got to pick two other friends to go on the date with the guys. I remember telling Jackie right before they announced the winners that if one of us won we shouldn't yell that we've won until the spokesperson had seen us. That way no one would try to steal our winning tickets. What can I say fangirls were crazy, loveable but crazy none-the-less. Jackie nodded her head in agreement and then they announced the winners.

I remember clutching onto my chakra necklace that hung firmly around my neck. I was thinking positive and in a way meditating, tuning all of the screaming people and clapping hands out as I imagined myself winning. I imagined what it would feel like to win, and I remember telling myself that I had already won. That's when they announced the two girls that won, and there was one girl left who would get to go on the date with the boys. The once noisy room had gone silent and everyone waited for the final numbers to be called. Tevin's mom read off the tiny piece of red paper and everyone's eyes were glued to their tickets. When the winner was called the young girl calmly walked up to the stage confused. That's when everyone realized that it was the same girl who had won a date the first round.

*What are the odds?*

That's when Tevin's mom picked up another ticket and everyone simultaneously snapped their heads back to their tickets awaiting the final numbers to be called...again. This time they called what I thought was my number and I read the black digits over about three times before I realized I won! I WON! I WON! Everything I told Jackie had flew out the door, and I jumped up and down screaming "I WON!" I acted like some deranged fan, and in that moment that's exactly what I was, deranged. I ran up to the stage until Tevin's parents came into view and once they saw me a look of recognition spread across their faces and they grinned knowingly. Tevin's dad chuckled.

"Don't tell me you won." He joked playfully.

I smirked and handed my ticket to Tevin's mom who read my winning digits. She then smiled.

"Oh she won alright."

I was beyond happy and soon enough I made my way back over to Jackie who grinned.

"What happened to no screaming until the spokesperson's seen us?" She asked.

I laughed and shrugged my shoulders in response.

The guys had come out from backstage to do a meet and greet, and once they saw me they immediately grinned widely. They were all so sweet.

"Hey Essynce." said Laniel.

"Heeey." said Sevin. That's when Laniel reached across Sevin and tapped Tevin on the shoulder.

"Tev, look who it is." He said. Tevin's eyes met mine and he came over and hugged me.

"Hey Essynce." He said cheerfully.

"He remembered my name!" I thought. Being cool and remaining calm was requiring a lot of energy in that moment. I felt like I was having an adrenaline rush!

"Hey guys!" I responded. "Guess what?"

"What?" Laniel asked.

"I won the raffle!"

"Seriously?" Sevin grinned.

I nodded my head enthusiastically. We were all smiling, and that's when we realized that there was a line of teenage girls behind me who were looking to have their turn at meeting the guys. So, we took a couple of pictures, and I left the meet and greet area.

I was beyond happy going home that day, and I couldn't wait to be reunited with the boys once again.

It was Monday and a couple of days since the concert. My mom told me that Tevin's mom texted her and said the date had been scheduled. I was super excited! I had a hard time deciding which friends would get to go on the date with me. Amy's mom would say no, I knew that for a fact, and Alice didn't like the guys. She said, and I quote "They're too attractive. How could I go on a date with someone so...*pretty*?" I laughed at her response and decided to ask my friends Jackie and Alex, they both agreed to come. We were all pumped for the date. Then, a day or two later I was informed by my mom that the date would be rescheduled because one of the guys had lost a relative. I didn't freak out or anything. In fact, I was more worried about how the guys were holding up. They were like one big family so if one of them was upset they all would be effected. I couldn't help but feel sorry for their loss.

About a week later, Jackie, Alex, and I went to my mom's car after school. We all thought I had an interview, and the people interviewing me wanted to meet some of my friends. So, there we were in the midst of other kids at my school, and once we turned the corner to where the corner store was (the same store the fight was in chapter two) I saw Tevin's sister, Vexi holding a camera recording.

I was confused.

Then out of the corner store came Tevin, Sevin, and Laniel holding balloons and small, adorable teddy bears. Jackie, Alex, and I were freaking out! I heard Amy mutter "Oh my god" behind us and I knew it was all too good to be true, but it was true. It was real and it was absolutely amazing! Tevin held a poster with my name on it with words like "Tevin's Girl" and "Mrs. Tevin Zordon" written in tiny words around my name. I hugged all of them and gladly accepted my balloons, poster, and teddy bear from Tevin. I then turned to Jackie and Alex to see that they received their gifts as well. Then, out of nowhere an avalanche of 12 and 13-year-old girls poured out of the school building, and turned the corner only to come face to face with the guys. I went over to greet Tevin's parents along with Vexi. We made small talk and laughed quietly at all the reactions from my schoolmates at seeing the guys, and my surprised reaction when I saw the boys come out of the store. There was crying and screaming, and the boys from my school either looked confused, envious, or slightly angry.  I mean, the majority of the female populations' attention was on these three teenage boys.


It was actually entertaining.


After taking a bunch of pictures, and meeting a bunch of my associates the guys and everyone else they came with got into their cars. My mom told me we would be meeting them at the mall.  When we got to the mall Jackie, Alex, and I changed out of our school uniforms into the outfits we thought we were wearing to the interview, which we knew now was only a part of surprising us.  I wore a flannel, black crop top, black pants, and timberlands. Jackie wore a multi-colored flannel, jeans, and sneakers. Finally, Alex wore a cute military green jacket, jeans, and sneakers.  We took a bunch of pictures of our outfits. Meanwhile, a bunch of girls at our school, some we have never spoken to, sent us multiple texts and called us several times about the guys.  I had 6th graders texting me and asking if I could ask the guys questions, asking where we all were, and I noticed that Jackie and Alex were getting the same texts and calls.  We all laughed and put our phones on silent.  We were gonna enjoy this day with no interruptions.

We met up with the guys at Applebee's in the mall. Once we got there they greeted us and made room in the seating booths.  I sat between Tevin and Laniel on one side, and Jackie and Alex sat on either side of Sevin on the other. That's when Laniel asked Sevin,

"Isn't there something you wanted to show the girls?"

At first Sevin looked confused, then he caught on to whatever Laniel was getting at and he responded with,

"Oh yeah right."

Next thing we know Sevin takes a steak knife off the table and does the knife challenge. He began singing a song with one hand flat on the table, fingers spread, and the knife in the other. As Sevin sang he jabbed the knife in between his fingers to the beat of the song. The girls and I were silent, watching in fear that he'd stab himself, and undeniably interested to see how the event would play out. The faster Sevin sang the faster he'd jab at the spaces in between his fingers with the knife. Laniel and Tevin were grinning obviously entertained as they watched their friend do the challenge, but they weren't at all nervous like we were. "Sevin must do this often" I thought.

After we ordered our food, and Sevin successfully completed the knife challenge without injuring himself we began roaming around the mall. We went to a bunch of stores and took a bunch of pictures. It was fun and I still couldn't believe it was real. The guys were like big kids. They had loads of energy and would literally run to their favorite stores. All I could do was laugh. When we went into stores the guys would ask me for fashion advice like, what looked best with what, and what was worth getting. They bought A LOT of stuff, and it was all really nice too. I couldn't lie, they had great taste in clothing and they paid for all of it with their own money. A few hours passed and it was time to go. We hugged, said our goodbyes, and left.

It was around 7:30pm and I asked my mom if the girls and I could go to the PAL. She dropped us off, and about half-an-hour later Jackie got picked up by her mom. We ran into Zach and he let Alex and I borrow his bike to go to the corner store. We took turns riding the bike, and on our way back Alex rode as I sat on the metal in between the handle bars and Alex. It was risky but exhilarating. We crossed streets as the evening air blew into my face, I felt alive. We talked about the date, and what the favorite part was for each of us. I even named the teddy bear Tevin had given me. I named it Tevin Jr.

*I know. Sooo creative, right?*

Eventually, our magical day had come to an end, and Alex and I walked to my house. She was picked up soon after. Once I got to my room I did one of those typical movie moments when the girl jumps on the bed, looks at the ceiling, and sighs. I had a good day. No, a great one.

The following week at school I brought Tevin Jr with me every day as a reminder of Tevin and all the fun we had at the mall. Everyone knew exactly who the teddy bear was from. The Tevin Zordon himself. The whole school knew the guys had come on Friday to surprise me.

Around the time of my store's grand-opening, back in November, a rumor had spread that I was going out with Tevin. I didn't deny it nor did I say it was true. However, the fire on that rumor only seemed to ignite after they surprised me at the school.

I remember one day that same week at lunch Tevin Jr sat in my lap as I ate. "The Flame" looked at the bear intently, obviously in deep thought and then he asked me a question that I didn't expect at all.


"If I got you a bear would you carry it around like that?"

Everyone heard what he said and at first I was too surprised to even respond. Did I hear him correctly?

"I don't know." Was all I said. Why would he ask me that? Oh my god...was he jealous?

# Notes:

----------------

# Chapter 9:

# "Nothing Could Bring Me Down..."

----------------

# Chapter 9
## *"Nothing Could Bring Me Down..."*

*G*rowing up I received countless awards for many things. For example; karate tournaments, talent shows, and entrepreneurial excellence. What I've come to know is that it isn't always about what you get, but it's about who you share it with and inspire. On December 9th, in the year 2015 I got to share something great with some really awesome people.

After school, I rounded up some friends to accompany me to my store to celebrate as I received an award from the senator of New Jersey. My mom's friend, who I had known since I was a baby, her son (my god-brother), who had to be about 6 years old at the time came to give some of my friends a lift to the store. Alice, Alex, Jackie, Amy, "The Flame", Zach, and DJ came.

When we got to my store the senator and a group of important looking people wearing black and grey suits greeted us at the door. After they finished making small talk with my staff, my friends took a seat as I shook many hands and put names to different faces. They congratulated me on my accomplishments and gifted me with a proclamation that the senator read aloud in front of everyone that was there. That included my parents, my grandad and his wife, my friends, my staff, and the people in those fancy suits.

I remember being so happy, so confident, and when the senator had finished reading I couldn't help but notice that "The Flame" was one of the first to clap for me. Everyone looked so proud of me and it was an amazing feeling. I was proud of myself. When the senator and the others had left, my friends and I went to the back of my store while the adults conversed in the front.

There, in the back of my store we goofed off and cracked jokes. My friends each congratulated me and then we found a microphone. "The Flame" took the microphone and gave me a shoutout only to break out into karaoke. He sang and sang until all of us were on the floor dying from laughter. IT WAS HILARIOUS! Then out of nowhere he began saying how he was an entrepreneur as well, and when he was asked to spell entrepreneur he refused. Everyone had laughed, including the adults and when my god-brother needed help on his homework "The Flame" did it for him. I told him to make his handwriting sloppy so it would be believable. He nodded in agreement and asked my 6-year-old god-brother if he had a girlfriend in which my god-brother responded,

"Yea, two."

I shook my head while laughing and said that was terrible. Meanwhile, "The Flame" complimented him and gave him high fives as if he won a metal.

"Don't encourage it." I said elbowing him.

"The Flame" only responded by displaying his evil, dimpled, grin. *Fryck.*

Afterwards, I suggested to "The Flame" that he and I should have a handshake. He nodded, took my hand, and ended up creating the whole thing. We still use it too, waiting for the day one of us forgets it.

When it was time to go, my friends and I made our way into my mom's truck. We all spoke about our favorite memories with each other, and reminisced over how we all met. We sang along to the songs that played on the radio, and my mom engaged in our conversation as well which didn't bother me at all. My friends loved her, and she loved them whether or not she ever cared to admit it. When everyone was home safely my mom and I went home.

When I went into my room I inserted the passcode on my phone and scrolled through all the pictures we had taken that day. I even posted a few of them. That's when I remembered that I needed to feed my guinea pigs. I usually fed them after school, but I wasn't able to earlier since I left to go to my store. I had two guinea pigs, Cinnamon and Skunky. They were both girls and I had them since I was eight, so for almost six years and counting. As I made my way downstairs, I thought about all the great things that had occurred that day. My friends being there for me, my award, and I even got to spend some time bonding with "The Flame."

"Today was great." I thought.

"Nothing could bring me down at this point." I thought.

That's when I looked into the guinea pig cage to greet Cinnamon and Skunky but…she was dead.

Cinnamon was dead.

# Notes:

-------------

# Chapter 10:
# "Thanks A Lot Cinnamon"

-------------

# Chapter 10
## *"Thanks A Lot Cinnamon"*

**Y**ou ever feel like you can never be *too* happy? It's like if you let yourself get *too* happy that you just know something's gonna go wrong. Somehow you know the world is going to find some way to prove to you that your happiness is only temporary. In other words, it won't last forever. That's what I learned that day on December 9th, that my happiness would only ever be temporary.

I felt like I'd taken ten steps forward and eight steps back. Cinnamon's death had become a symbolic reminder that I could never be engulfed in 100% happiness, and if I ever succeeded in doing so something horrible would happen. I still feel that way today. I remember being paralyzed, in absolute shock as I stared at her limp corpse and open dead eyes. She had absolutely no signs of life in her, no breathing, no twitching, nothing. My mom's boyfriend, Michael removed her remains out of the cage because I didn't have it in me to touch her. A horrified Skunky was left in the midst of everything. Skunky looked so frightened, so fearful and I felt like it was my fault. Like I had done something wrong.

That's when I had gone back to not wanting to care. I told myself that I shouldn't. *"She was only a guinea pig"* I thought. Cinnamon wasn't a cat or a dog, not even a bird. She was a four-legged rodent that most considered to be a disgusting rat. As much as I tried to see her that way too, I couldn't. Cinnamon was there before there was an Essynce Couture. She was there before the fake friends, heartbreaks, and letters being put into math. She reminded me of such a simpler time, my childhood in its glory. The good old days. Now she was gone, and all that simplicity and "easy going" exterior had seem to go with her.

I started overthinking a lot. Everything had become a "what if" or "do I really think this is gonna work out?" I questioned everything, myself, my happiness, and my life.

*Why was I here?*

*Why could I never win entirely?*

*Did I not deserve greatness?*

And to think this was all because a disgusting rat had died on the best day ever. It was the start of a never-ending battle in my head between optimism and pessimism.

After that day, I never let myself get *too* happy. When something good would happen I would enjoy it, but my joy would be limited because I feared I would play a role in something bad that I just knew would take place if I got too happy, too lost in the moment. I thought this burden would be thrust upon my shoulders, and I would be the only one to blame. It hurt and I had a hard time understanding why it did so much. So, every time something phenomenal would occur I would hear a little voice in the back of my mind say, "Relax, don't get too happy." Then there'd be all this happiness and joy and this little undeniable feeling of despair that I just couldn't shake.

*Thanks a lot Cinnamon.*

# Notes:

Essynce E. Moore

**■ ■ ■ ■ ■ ■ ■ ■ ■ ■ ■ ■**

# Chapter 11:
# "This Generation Is A Walking Petty Party"

**■ ■ ■ ■ ■ ■ ■ ■ ■ ■ ■ ■**

# Chapter 11
## *"This Generation Is A Walking Petty Party"*

**W**ord had spread about some new girl who would be transferring to our school. She wasn't just *"some new girl."* No, she was a *celebrity*. At least that's what you'd expect her to be judging by the amount of time people spent talking about her arrival. It was incredibly, enormously, and painfully annoying! Every day for about two weeks people spoke of this 13 year old girl as if she were responsible for world peace. Till this day, her two-syllable name is imbedded in my brain as if someone stamped it there with permanent ink. Now don't get me wrong, I didn't have a problem with the girl. I didn't even know her, but when you hear about one person and one person only for two weeks straight, trust me, you get annoyed. When the girl had arrived at school all the talk about her seemed to die down, and believe me I was thankful. That is until her name appeared again. Somehow, she'd gotten herself involved in our school's drama as if she were adapting to a new, petty environment. Girls felt threatened because she was indeed pretty and boys, like Dre, flirted with her as if it were their job to do so. However, I couldn't help but think she succeeded in blending in with everyone else.

I had come to the conclusion that her, along with all the other humans in my school had fallen into the same habits and tendencies. It was like everyone was just another copy of the person standing next to them. There was no individuality what so ever. Everyone talked the same, argued the same, and people even dressed the same! It was like our generation had fallen into a bubble and everyone had adapted to having the same style and attitude to go with it. Now I knew it wasn't everyone but I did know that it wasn't easy spotting people who stood out attitude and fashion wise. It seemed like everybody was trying to be the same kind of *unique* in their own repetitive, recurring way.

---

At the end of December my good friend Ava invited me to her birthday party and I was excited! Parties were never really my thing, but I always managed to find ways to have fun. Fun was a must!

When I arrived at Ava's house I realized just how many people she had invited. There had to be around 30 of us in her basement, but I wasn't complaining. In fact, I knew most of them. Once I walked in everyone greeted me, yelling over the loud music. I saw Jonas and James (from chapter 4) and greeted Jonas first. Then I made my way to James who was already on his way to me. As I walked towards him I couldn't help but smile. Literally, I could not stop smiling. Why couldn't I stop smiling?! James wore a multi-colored hoodie and jeans. He looked the same since I had last seen him when we were playing football. When we finally were in each other's presence he picked me up with the same cheesy grin on his face and spun me around. I laughed the whole time. When he put me down I lost him in the crowd, and that's when I really got to take in my surroundings. There really were a lot of people and Ava had a pretty good set up. There was a table with a bunch of snacks such as candy, chips, pizza, and sooo much more. That right there was enough for me to have a good time.

Near the candy was a pile of colorful glo sticks. As I reached out to grab a purple one a hand stopped me. That's when I looked up and saw who the hand belonged to, James. He chuckled and told me to look at the sticky notes on the table. I hadn't noticed them before but when I saw them I laughed. The glo sticks were color-coded and each color had a sticky note under it that identified what each color meant. Blue was taken, green was single, and purple was "it's complicated." I grabbed a green one (single teenagers unite!) and asked James to help me put it on. He took the glo stick and fumbled with the plastic end that he connected to the other, around my wrist like a bracelet. As he wrapped the neon plastic around my wrist I couldn't help but wonder what color was wrapped around his. Was it blue or green? Those were the two colors everyone seemed to be wearing the most, especially green. My eyes managed to find themselves on James' arm and I have to admit, the color did sort of catch me off guard. It was purple. I didn't know whether to ask him about it or laugh but then again, why did I care?  Oh, I knew why, it was because I had a tiny crush on James.  That's why.

The party continued and everyone danced to the music and ate the food.  That food had no chance.  The room was dark enough for you to see everyone's glo sticks and there was enough light for you to see who everyone was.  I forced a stubborn James to dance, and soon after we went into a room with a couple of other people to play video games.  His subtle flirting didn't go unnoticed by me either.

When the party was over, my mom picked me up around 11:45pm.  I was one of the last to go.  When I got home I went onto James' Instagram and within the first three recent posts I saw there was a video.  I clicked on it and there, on my phone screen, was a video of James making out with some girl.

*"Typical guy."* I thought.

I guess you can say that put me in a semi-petty mood and I couldn't resist the urge to comment on the post...so I did.  Under the long list of comments posted by people talking about how cute they were and a never-ending series of heart-eye emojis, I allowed my pettiness to purge by using one single word.

I commented, "Goals" with the little lock and key emoji.  For some reason my 13-year-old self was incredibly satisfied and happy with my response.  Thinking about it now I find it hilarious!

Moments later my comment was deleted.  James deleted my comment.

HAHAHAHAHAHAHAHAHAHAHAHAHAHAHAHAHAHAHA HAHAHAHAHA

THIS GENERATION IS A WALKING PETTY PARTY!!! HAHAHA

# Notes:

# Chapter 12:

# "I Have No Choice Other Than To..."

# Chapter 12
## *"I Have No Choice Other Than To..."*

$\mathcal{M}$y friend Zach and I had been best friends since 6th grade. We told each other pretty much everything, and even though we had our differences we always seemed to come together in the end. We were sort of like siblings.

Sometime in December Zach texted me and it was a text that worried me. It read,

"Bad news."

"What??" I responded.

"I'm moving."

"What do you mean? Where?"

"Florida..."

And in that moment, I cried. Some may say I overreacted and others may laugh. The point is I felt like I was losing one of the only few people I could trust, the person I could tell everything to, and finally the one person who knew exactly what to say when I was upset. That person was Zach. It had always been Zach.

I remember, going into my mother's room with tears in my eyes when I told her Zach was moving. She hugged me and told me that it would all be okay, and eventually it was.

Zach and I never got to say goodbye in person. He left way sooner than we thought he would. We texted often and he made me promise not to forget about him. A few months later I had an event in Florida and I got to surprise him. We walked around in Miami, went swimming, and caught up on everything going on in each other's lives. Sometimes I envied Zach's life. He was so easy going. There was never any drama and he always seemed to make friends easily. Zach was always so simple minded. If you wanted to do something but were scared to Zach would just tell you to do it anyway and that was that. There was no overthinking or being dramatic with Zach. It was either you live life or you don't. He always made the solutions to problems seem so simple and direct. That's partly why I appreciated him so much. He didn't sugar coat things, he just said what never crossed your mind. Zach and I are still best friends and one day we'll reunite all over again, but until that day comes I have no choice other than to miss him.

# Notes:

# Chapter 13:
# "A GTA God"

# Chapter 13
## *"A GTA God"*

𝒞hristmas time was approaching, and I asked my dad for a PS4 and the game GTA (Grand Theft Auto). Everyone in my school played, mostly the boys, and I was curious as to what the hype was all about so I asked for the game. I told some of my guy friends like "The Flame", DJ, and Jonas.  At first I wasn't sure if I wanted a PlayStation or XBOX, but the majority said PlayStation so that's what I got.

My first experience with my new game was fun. My friend Alec, who usually hung out with "The Flame" and his click taught me all there was to know about GTA and my PS4.  He taught me how to fight, rob stores in the game, and different ways to make money.  He gave me tips on who and who not to accept as a friend request, and I even let him pick my character's name on GTA. Sometimes we'd fight to see who would win and for a long time he always beat me, but soon enough I started beating him. He would laugh and tell other guys that I could beat them too. Alec was a great player. We played almost every day, and like a forest fire the word spread that I had gotten the game and my PS4.

When I went to school all the guys there asked me for my screen name so they could add me. They asked what games I had and what level I was on. Many of them suggested games and hacks I could use when playing. It was like I joined this alternate gaming universe where everyone played games and exchanged gaming secrets. It was kind of awesome!

I told "The Flame" I had gotten the PS4 and he told me he already knew. Someone told him and not long after we accepted each other's friend request. Now Alec was a great player and everyone knew that, but "The Flame"... he was treated like a GTA god. It was a fact and no one denied knowing that either. When we played, for some reason he took it easy on me, unless I challenged him and I didn't win too many of those battles. We talk to each other through the headset that came with the game, and sometimes our conversations would last all night. Sometimes it would have nothing to do with the game at all. One day, after a snowstorm, I came outside to help my mom put some stuff in the car. I was in my pajamas. Across the street was Dre, DJ, this guy Seon, and "The Flame". They were shoveling my neighbor's drive way and when "The Flame" saw me he crossed the street, and the first thing he said to me was, "You look like you've been up all night playing GTA." I laughed. I knew he was right. I was wearing fuzzy pants, a cropped hoodie, flip flops, and my grey dreads were all over the place. I spent the whole night playing video games, and for the first time I understood why guys never text back. It was like once you started playing the world just slipped away from you. The screen in front of you was the world, and it was so easy to lose track of time. Yet I liked it, I was thoroughly enjoying this new hobby of mine.

# Notes:

Essynce E. Moore

--- --- --- --- --- --- --- --- --- --- --- --- ---

# Chapter 14:
# "Friends"

--- --- --- --- --- --- --- --- --- --- --- --- ---

# Chapter 14
## *"Friends"*

*e*very celebrity has fans, some more than others but fans none-the-less. They're supposed to be those people who support you regardless of your mistakes, those who love you, and will do anything to see you succeed. At least I thought that's just what they were, but I have come to know that they weren't just supporters they were so much more...

Sometime in January I met this girl, I don't remember what grade she was in but I do remember she was younger than me. Her name was Maggie. When I first met Maggie I could tell she was nervous to talk to me, but I couldn't understand why. I mean why would anybody be nervous to talk to *me*? I wasn't Beyoncé or that woman from all those Progressive commercials. I'd gone to that school for three years, and everybody knew me so there was no reason for Maggie to be scared to talk to me. She acted as if she were afraid to say the wrong thing but she didn't, not once. She told me that I was her role model, she looked up to me, and I motivated her to achieve her dreams. I was speechless, incredibly surprised and...happy. I thanked and hugged Maggie because I didn't hear those things in school too often, and it really meant a lot. Sometimes, Maggie would bring me gifts. Gifts like this mini statue of an angel because she said I reminded her of one, and she would write me letters that said the sweetest things. Soon she began sitting with me at lunch and I introduced her to my friends. She asked us all for advice involving her and how she should handle issues with her friends. We all said something different, but she visibly appreciated what I had to say the most. Maggie wasn't just a fan, she became my friend.

Then, there was this other time I had asked to get a drink of water during class. When I left to go get water I greeted the security guard, who I've known all my years in middle school, who sat in the hallway on a plastic chair with metal legs. When I started making my way back to class a voice behind me said my name causing me to stop in my tracks.

"Essynce?" The voice said. This voice sounded uncertain, almost as if it were asking if it was me rather than knowing for sure. This young and childlike voice, mimicked the sound of an 11-year-old boy and it sounded like it was hoping it was me, like I was the answer to all the world's problems. When I turned around I came face to face to a kid, who was definitely younger than me. He was cute in a "aww he's adorable" sort of way and he was much shorter than me. His face lit up like a Christmas tree when he saw that it was me, and he ran up and hugged me screaming "It's you! It's you! You're the one on the book!"

My grin matched his and before I could say the word fryck we were both smiling uncontrollably. The boy than turned to the security guard and said cheerfully "It's her! She's the one who wrote the book!" The security guard responded with a calm yet amused "I know" and then looked at me with the same expression. He couldn't believe that it was me, and I couldn't believe how happy he was. When we parted ways and I had to get back to class as I walked away I heard him say "Bye Essynce" enthusiastically as if he'd been dying to call me by my name the entire time. Soon after that we started seeing each other pretty often in school, and he always looked happy to see me. Last I saw him he refused to hug me because he said and I quote had a girlfriend who was standing right next to him and I nodded in understanding. It was charming and incredibly adorable. He didn't want his girlfriend to see him hugging another girl. He was going to make a great husband haha!

Finally, there was this other girl in my school. She was a year younger than me, and she first reached out to me through Instagram. She told me how much I inspired her to write a book about her life. She informed me all about herself and what she has been through growing up. I could tell just how strong she was. She wanted to share her story rather than cower away from it. I ended up reading some of her writing that was given to me, and I gave her the best critique I could. She was so sweet and funny. She made you smile when you were around her, and we ended up texting quite a bit. She became a great friend of mine without a doubt.

Anyway, my point is "fans" aren't just your supporters. They're people who stand by your side, and mean a lot to you. You don't just make them happy, they make you happy and sometimes they're there when you need them most. On those days you need some cheering up or just a reason to smile they are always there, waiting patiently just to see you happy. My fans are my friends, and I wouldn't trade them for anything. They are not people you want to lose!

# Notes:

----------------

# Chapter 15: "I'm So Different."

----------------

# Chapter 15
## *"I'm So Different."*

*Y*ou ever take a minute to look up, above all the stereotypes, above all the drama, and beyond all that is in front of you?  Towards the end of the school year, I did.  I looked up...and it was weird.

One day at lunch, just like any other I simply wasn't in the mood to talk so I just listened to everyone else talk.  While I listened, I couldn't help but feel odd.  To my right girls were talking about Instagram, to my left boys were talking about recent fights that took place, and right in front of me people talked about who they thought the most attractive people were in the school.  That's when I began to think...*I'm so different*.  I could care less about Instagram updating their filters, people fighting over things that weren't worth fighting for, and who the "most attractive" people were in the school.  My mind was all about my future, what I was gonna do when I got out of that brainwashing building, and where I was gonna go first when I set seas to travel the world. My mind was different.

I entertained myself by getting lost in the thought of the roles I was gonna play in movies someday and the stories I was gonna write, about opposites attracting and ghost haunting. However, at the time, I didn't see these differences as gifts and something to be happy about. I saw them as obstacles, refusing to let me be like everyone else. I wanted to be unique, but not *too* unique. I wanted to stand out but not *too* much, and that's what these differences prevented me from doing. I couldn't shine in the light that I wanted to shine in...if that makes any sense.

So, there I was looking up and above all of the stereotypes and drama that was in front of me. I'm sure it sounds nice and eye-opening, but at the time it kind of sucked. I felt like an outcast, like no one could see things the way I saw them and it made me feel weird. I felt like a loner with a bunch of friends. Friends, who knew nothing about me, nothing about who I was, and what I wanted to do and I wasn't blaming anyone other than myself. I was a stranger in my own body. I thought something was wrong with me, like I had some disorder that prevented me from being *normal*. I didn't talk much in school after that, and because I didn't talk I was forced to listen to the idiocy that surrounded me. I felt cornered, like I couldn't escape the way these people thought, and the power their ignorance had over me. The things I heard them say only made it worse. In my head, I was screaming. I'd think to myself

*"I don't care!"*

*"How many times is she going to say that?"*

*"Why does it matter?"*

*"They do know middle school doesn't last a lifetime, right?"*

These thoughts would cloud my mind and push me into thinking that I was at fault. I thought my differences were the problem. The simple minded lived so simply and I envied them until one day...something clicked.

I was weird. I was different. I was unique and I loved myself because of it. My differences made me who I am. I was creative, crazy intelligent, and super diverse. I could see things in so many different perspectives. I managed to try and understand everyone in the best way I could. I found ways to befriend people who were nothing like me. I even found ways to be happy with my weird, loner mind. My mom once told me that people call weird what they can't understand, and I couldn't agree more. Most did not understand me because I was a book written in a foreign language very few were able to comprehend. I was a story that only I could tell, and I was so happy with who I was that I just stopped. I stopped caring about what people thought of me, and about "being normal" and that's when I thought why would I wanna be like everybody else anyway? I am awesome!

# Notes:

# Chapter 16: "Honestly"

# Chapter 16
## *"Honestly"*

*T*he school year would soon be over, but before it ended entirely we had two major events everyone had been looking forward to since 6th grade. These events would ensure we left middle school with a bang! We would be leaving our mark as the middle school class of 2016. The events were social and graduation.

Now for those who don't know, social was like a middle school prom. All the 8th graders would get to leave school early to get dressed up, and make their way towards the venue where the dance would take place. All middle schoolers dreamed of this day. We looked forward to it almost as much as we looked forward to graduation. The day of social we all got to dress down, meaning we didn't have to wear our uniforms. Most of the girls already had their nails painted while some waited for their parents to pick them up to take them to get ready. Girls wore bonnets to keep their hair prepped and ready for the dance, and boys wore doo rags to get their waves in check for the occasion. During the day everyone looked a mess. We all wore sweatpants and baggy clothes just to make sure our glo-up that night would be tremendous!

When my mom picked me up to get ready it was around 12:30 in the afternoon, and the dance started at 6:30 PM. So, we had plenty of time to get ready. Once we left the school we began walking towards our car, and we saw a bunch of my other friends getting picked up by their parents for the same exact reason. We all had goofy smiles on our faces, and we couldn't wait for the night to arrive. When my mom and I made it to the car we went to my store so I could get ready. Once my hair, nails, and make-up was done we drove home where my family waited patiently outside. My aunt and my cousin help me get my dress and jewelry together. My mentor helped too. I felt like I was getting married, and everyone was helping me prepare for the ceremony.

I wore a purple and gold Essynce Couture dress with a headpiece I had specially made for the occasion. I also wore gladiator heels and gold jewelry. I resembled royalty. That was the look I was going for.

My mom spoke with another one of my cousins outside who would be escorting me to social on a motorcycle along with his friends. My grandad lent us his Mercedes for me to ride in, and once I was ready I stepped outside only to be attacked by cameras being held by my relatives. We took pictures in the street with all the motorcycles and bikers forcing general traffic to drive around us. I remember this girl in the passenger seat of a car staring at me in awe, and mouthing to me "You look so pretty." I said thank you and I remember feeling something like an adrenaline rush. I was super excited and I couldn't wait to arrive at the dance.

When we got in my grandad's Mercedes to leave, my dad drove and my mom sat in the passenger seat. The motorcycles surrounded the car the whole way to the venue like they do for presidents in the movies, and when I arrived I had an epic grand entrance. Multiple parents stood outside taking pictures, and some of the high-schoolers were there too to support their friends. My friend Faith, who didn't go to our school was there, and when she saw me she immediately whipped out her phone to record my entrance. I had a biker on each arm, and they escorted me into the venue while another held the train of my dress. It was pretty dramatic if you ask me, but hey it wouldn't be me if it wasn't over the top.

The minute I stepped into the room where the event took place about five of my guy friends surrounded me like sharks, but I wasn't their prey. I was their muse. I received compliment after compliment from them and I was very flattered. The night was already off to a good start. After meeting up with a bunch of my friends and taking so many pictures we all made our way to the dance floor. They served food, but no one sat down long enough to really enjoy it. The few bites I had it wasn't half bad. When they brought out desert no one noticed...but I did. There was chocolate, vanilla, and strawberry ice cream on everyone's plate, but no one bothered to notice since they were all on the dance floor. However, ice cream was my all-time weakness and I couldn't help but take not one, not two, but three plates of ice cream off of someone's table, including my own. I didn't feel bad about it one bit. It was delicious! When the night came to an end most of us went to Applebee's, including me, and we reminisced about our social experience that we were convinced topped all the others. I honestly don't think that will be a day many of us will forget.

---

Graduation day was...hectic. Everyone looked great and happy but I wasn't. My nails were messed up, my hair was nothing like I'd wanted it to be, and at the time I hated my dress. I just wanted the whole thing to be over with. I even wore sunglasses so people couldn't see what I was really feeling. I felt annoyed and irritated all because this day was going nothing like I planned. When the ceremony was over I took pictures because I knew I'd regret it if I didn't, and by the time I finished I couldn't wait to leave. When we left I got to pick where we would eat to celebrate. I don't remember where we went, but I do remember running into some familiar faces there. One of them belonging to "The Flame". I laughed at the irony that we both ended up in the same place and he did as well. It was cute to see him there with his family, and when we parted, I went to mine.

---

If you asked me how I liked the 8<sup>th</sup> grade, I would ask you if you wanted the truth. If you said yes, I'd say that 8<sup>th</sup> grade, in a nutshell, kind of sucked. I had more bad times than good, and more nightmares than dreams come true. However, I wouldn't trade it for anything because I learned sooo much! I learned about myself, what I want from the world, and what I want from my life. I learned about what a real friend is and what it's like to be one. I learned about what my interest are and what I can't stand. Knowledge is never not worth knowing, and everything I learned will come in handy someday. I know that for sure. What's crazy about it all is that I don't remember a single thing one of my teacher's taught me, but I do remember most of what my experiences have done. In conclusion, if you can take only one thing out of this book just remember that life is about learning, and if you can do that, you can live through anything and everything!

## THE END

# Notes:

# 8<sup>th</sup> Grade Middle School Chronicles

## The year that changed everything...

## Written by

# Essynce E. Moore

# Essynce Moore's Bio

## The Fashionista

Essynce Moore started designing clothes at the tender age of 6 with just for fun doodles in her school binder and notepads.  Her passion was and still is, to find her own style and to share her creative UPSCALE clothing ideas and styles with youth around the world. Essynce is a "TEEN" that has turned her passion into a business for 2013, with the launch of her official clothing line branded Essynce Couture, LLC with the motto *"a child's passion for fashion."*  Essynce Couture also has a natural body product line for children, tweens, and teens labeled "Wynk" by Essynce Couture.  In 2015 Essynce launched Essynce Couture Spa and Boutique EXCLUSIVELY for Children, Tweens, and Teens to give the youth a place of their own to visit and be pampered, inspired, and educated.

Essynce is an entrepreneur, child's fashion designer/stylist, author, actress, celebrity, motivational speaker, and fashionista that brings a positive vibe to her peers and others. She's been in numerous fashion shows, pageants, karate tournaments and has spoken at numerous conferences and/or workshops. In 2016-17 Essynce is in the following movies: Best of 2 Evils, King of Newark, Custody, Darker than Blue – Colin Warner Project, and Maggie's Plan. She has SHOWCASED at both NY Fashion Weeks and Atlanta Kids Fashion Week while also ripping the runway. She's released her first book 6th Grade Middle School Chronicles in 2015 and her 2nd book 7th Grade Middle School Chronicles in 2016. She has been featured on BET, Verizon Fios News, BlackNews.com, MadameNoire, The Record newspaper, The Epoch Times newspaper, and a host of other news and media outlets. Essynce has also been awarded 2016 Teenpreneur of the Year by Black Enterprise, as well as, awarded by the City of Passaic with a Proclamation, and awarded by the State of New Jersey – Senate and General Assembly upon the auspicious occasion of the Grand Opening of her business Essynce Couture Spa and Boutique, LLC in 2015 in the City of Passaic. In 2014 she was interviewed and featured on NBC (Channel 4 News), Jeff Foxx of WBLS FM, BuzzFeed, Yahoo, Verizon Fios Channel 1 News, NBC Channel 4 News, she was awarded "2014 Young Emerging Leader" by Alpha Kappa Alpha, she's been featured in the 2013 TIME for Kids Magazine, Honored 2013 Entrepreneur of the Year by the Vashti School for Future Leaders, she's been seen on the Uncle Majic Commercial (BET, VH1, Channel 11, etc), HBO (Bored to Death), and has involved herself with a host of other events and projects.

Essynce is also a member of the New York Youth Chamber of Commerce (NYYCC).

This young "phenomenon" is *BUZZING* and she can't wait to see children being pampered, as well as, wearing her Essynce Couture brand all around the world.

# The Essynce Couture Brand

***What makes us unique?!?*** Essynce Couture, LLC is one of the 1st children's clothing lines designed by a child with "education" in mind. We focus on styling our clothes to compliment all sizes, races, and colors of all children around the world. In addition, we offer great incentives through our Essynce Couture membership program to the children who support Essynce Couture, LLC by allowing them the opportunity to show and prove. They can upload either their report cards, certificates, awards or any other form of achievement(s) to one of the Essynce Couture social networks (instagram, twitter, or facebook) and may be selected to be rewarded by Essynce Couture, LLC incentives. This will encourage children to continue to do well in school and remind them that education is very important, rewarding, stylish, and can be fun!

www.essyncecouture.com

# Notes:

CPSIA information can be obtained
at www.ICGtesting.com
Printed in the USA
LVHW08s1046141018
593523LV00008BA/360/P